no
ordinary
place

OTHER BOOKS
BY PAMELA PORTER

I'll Be Watching,
Groundwood Books, 2011

This Awakening to Light,
Leaf Press, 2010

Cathedral,
Ronsdale Press, 2010

The Intelligence of Animals,
The Backwaters Press, 2008

Yellow Moon, Apple Moon,
Groundwood Books, 2008

Stones Call Out,
Coteau Books, 2006

The Crazy Man,
Groundwood Books, 2005

Sky, Groundwood Books, 2004

Poems for the Luminous World,
Frog Hollow Press, 2002

no ordinary place

pamela porter

RONSDALE PRESS

RONSDALE PRESS
3350 West 21st Avenue
Vancouver, B.C., Canada V6S 1G7
www.ronsdalepress.com

Typesetting: Julie Cochrane, in New Baskerville 11 pt on 13.5
Cover Design: Julie Cochrane
Paper: Ancient Forest Friendly Silva — 100% post-consumer waste, totally chlorine-free and acid-free

Ronsdale Press wishes to thank the following for their support of its publishing program: the Canada Council for the Arts, the Government of Canada through the Canada Book Fund, the British Columbia Arts Council, and the Province of British Columbia through the Book Publishing Tax Credit Program.

Library and Archives Canada Cataloguing in Publication

Porter, Pamela, 1956–
    No ordinary place: poems/Pamela Porter.

Issued also in electronic format.
ISBN 978-1-55380-151-1

    I. Title.

PS8581.O7573N6 2012   C811'.6   C2011-906411-1

At Ronsdale Press we are committed to protecting the environment. To this end we are working with Canopy (formerly Markets Initiative) and printers to phase out our use of paper produced from ancient forests. This book is one step towards that goal.

Printed in Canada by Marquis Book Printing, Quebec, Canada

for Rob, Cecilia
and Drew

—

from no ordinary place
do we come, and there
will we find each other again

ACKNOWLEDGEMENTS

—

Acknowledgment is gratefully extended to the following publications in which some of these poems first appeared: *Arc, Cirque, CV2, FreeFall, Fiddlehead, Prairie Fire, Room, Tiferet, Vallum.*

The poem "My Father's Grief" won the 2010 *Vallum* Poetry Prize.

"A Table in the Wilderness" and "Like I Told You" first appeared in chapbooks published by Leaf Press, edited by Patrick Lane.

"Tenebrae" is the Latin word for "shadows." The twelve anthems of the Tenebrae service are sung on Maundy Thursday in the Orthodox tradition as the congregation keeps vigil throughout the night, waiting for the light to return.

"The Night of My Conception" was inspired by Lorna Crozier's two poems, "The Night of My Conception 1" and "The Night of My Conception 2," from her volume of poems, *What the Living Won't Let Go.* "The Restive Angel" was inspired by "What I Gave You, Truly" from *The Apocrypha of Light.*

"The Heart Is an Argument with Darkness" was inspired by Lorna Crozier's series of poems taken from lines in Patrick Lane's volume of poetry *A Linen Crow, A Caftan Magpie.* The lines used in this series are taken from *A Linen Crow, A Caftan Magpie,* and from *Too Spare, Too Fierce.*

I would like to thank Russell Thorburn for his help with the manuscript that became this book. His vision and intuitive logic are invaluable. Also, I wish to thank my fellow writers in the WayWords writing group, in the Ocean Wilderness and Honeymoon Bay retreats and at Planet Earth Poetry for their support and encouragement. Finally, with deepest gratitude I want to thank Lorna Crozier and Patrick Lane, my best and most beloved teachers and mentors.

CONTENTS

II

—

III

—

IV

—

AN OFFERING

—

Many bring food. Some carry flowers.
I've brought poems —

bouquets in profusion, armfuls,
a cacophonous disarray
the wind, magnanimous as a father,
sweeps into his arms,

petals strewn underfoot,
imprinted into mud, cleaved
to the soles of our shoes.

Many bring food. Others,
flowers. I've brought poems

for every season — of dreams born,
burning, broken, and the one
when, after protracted grief,

a scrap of melody begins
like a perilous grace —
                    dishevelled,
discordant as my frangible
offering, mud-smeared,

naked and tender and wanting.

Some bring food. It is
what they do at such times.
Others carry flowers.

I've brought you poems.

— I —

Branches, Early Spring

They had begun to whisper among themselves,
hesitant at first, but it was cold you see,
and had been months cold. They had begun
to whisper as the ice loosened and thinned
on the trough, as the moon's startled face
rose above the blackened hills. I heard them
whisper, but did not know the moment
they began, or the precise dawn
in which they wakened from their stiff
and dreamless sleep. I know only
the horses bowed their heads to thatch,
I pushed the wheelbarrow toward the fence
where thin shoots blushed with colour, and higher,
the trees' red sap set the sky on fire.

Blessing

To be blessed
said the leaf,
is to lie finished
in dark earth,
my edges starry
with frost.

To be blessed
said the branch,
is to stand naked
in winter sun,
my blood rushing gold
and singing.

To be blessed
said the gate,
is to be rusted open
so that all may pass:
deer, leaves, wind,
mice, God.

Begin Again

After lightning, after thunder broke
the darkness brooding over the sleeping houses,
after rain, in silence morning bloomed.
The grasses lay mudded, rose petals
littered the dirt, and in that quiet, a bird
tried her tentative song. The cat
set a paw outside the barn; the horses,
rumps shining, weary with running, stood steaming
as the sun, that minor god, peered
from behind the clouds
as if to make some proclamation.
Then the horses lowered their muzzles to the plain,
and it was the beginning of the world, again.

Cat

She'd come home at last
mewling all night on the porch,
runt bundle of wild
fright in her bones
from the owl
sweeping the dark,
and the uncouth cries
of her owlet young filling
the trees and the night
with the black bells
of their sound.
She'd come home,
some furred creature
swallowed up in her, but now
she's had enough of wild,
the open mouth, needle teeth
of that life;
she has brought us
a strangeness riding
in her eyes: a sky
of dark cloud built up,
and the pelting rain.

Making a Life

And wind, always wind rolled over the land,
pulling the clouds thin and grey.
We had to go out — in snow, in cold, no matter —
I lay the baby in her crib to let her sleep
or cry. Some part of the fence was down;
a deer, maybe, or one of the horses run into it
in the blizzarding dark, or the wind
had sheared it off, the post long rotted
but holding taut in the tension of barbed wire
until, like someone exhausted or dying,
it could no longer keep itself upright.
Wind watered my eyes, the razored barbs
cut my hands through gloves, the bleached
bones of grass bent with the weight
of snow. First we had to pull the rusted
staples out, then the wire off the post,
the hard wooden knot like a face
etched with pain. Then a new post to go in:
the pounding of the maul, my hands
holding the new post straight; I stood
unseeing but for a smear of colour, the tremble
in my bones when my husband hit it clean, each time
missing my hands, my wrists, the skin
exposed and fiery with frost. The chokecherry
beside the cattle guard bloomed with birds
feasting on the final fruit, one hawk
on the power line, patient and lonely,
our child in her crib and her dark hunger.
My prayer for her sleep. Then the wire, coiled
like a summer rattler, pulled snug with the claw
of the hammer I held in place, my feet braced
in snow hard as love, burrs catching on my socks,
sleet of tears stinging my face,

my hands just holding on, and my breasts
sudden with milk. And when we finished,
the birds scattering from the chokecherry,
we stepped into the house as her newborn wail
shattered the air, and I, stunned with cold
and crying, my breasts burning
and the milk coming down.

Window

Three years after I slipped back
                into the world,
I lay and studied the morning bones
of my hands opening,
                closing, my fleshy wings,
the house sunlit and silent as heaven.

A sudden *bang*, and I slid my feet
to the floor. A cardinal
had flown into the window, shattering
                the dawn.
Light curled in sleep on the snow.
The bones of trees tapped at the frozen
                waters of the sky.

My bald uncle was out in his ear-flap hat,
high-stepping in clumsy boots.
I breathed crystals onto the glass,
                my palms pressing the thin
                separation between us,
and watched his eyebrows turn to ash,
his gloved hand lift
                the blood-red bird

                motionless as the angels
in my Bible story book. Barefoot
in my flannel nightgown,
                faced with death,

I never forgot the darkness
in its eyes, shining
with the last thing it had seen
before tumbling through
        to the other side:

        that veil
I still knew, and knew
would not let me back,
my loneliness fresh, the bruising
        air of the world
stroking my strange new skin.

A Round, with Descant

My little soul, fluttering flame,
flies away when I sleep. She has
no fear of death, that dark ice
      floating between the stars.
She holds her infinity close
and won't let me see.

My little child who lives in me
lies awake each night
        and does not sleep.
Her ear attends to nomad birds
crying in their bones,
      the humming dust of heaven,
a voice behind the blackened moon
whispering
        This is not your home.

My loneliness speaks
in the rivers of my veins, again
and again asking its name.
        Remember,
I answer. Your name is *remember,*
it is *mist in the dawn.*
Your name, I say, is *little sparrow*
gleaning winter ground.

And my mother? My father?
They live deep in a forest
      I have not yet found.
My mother sews dawn to the sun,
my father unrolls the fabric
of the sky. Together, they shake out
the light of summer, fold it over
and over in winter.

After half a century of walking,
        I will cross a bridge
of fallen leaves to find them.
I will carry bread to them, the seeds
of stars, the worn shoes
        of desire.

I will stroke their heads and say,
I am here now, little Mother,
I heard you call in dream, Father,
and I will place my tenderness
in jars ancient and jade.

When they sit down to the table
I will feed them from my hands,
reaching down
        to the ripe fruit,
scraping each jar clean.

Another Word for Daughter

Another word for *daughter*
        is *remember.*
Remember ripples the still waters of childhood.
Remember walks abandoned roads,
        dust clinging to her shoes.

Another word for *mother*
        is *silence.*
Silence tucks the sheets around the child's bed.
Silence wanders in and out all the rooms of the house.

Other words for *daughter*
        are *stranger,* and *shadow* —
the child wakens in the night and knows
        she is a stranger
to those who sleep in the other rooms,
as *remember* and *silence* meet each other,
one on the top and one on the bottom stair.

Not even the geese know her, who pass in the sky
riding two long wings, their music
another word for *poverty,*
        which echoes
through the shadowed chambers of her heart.

And another way to say *heart*
is to say, *little drum beating*
        under the moon.
And another way to say *moon*
is to say, *blue crayon circle*
        caught in night's branches.

And another way to say *night*
is to say, *remember* —
      the ruddied face of the moon
she reaches for,

      a memory
of those who loved her
before she became human again,
      snagged in the branches
of her bones, the radiant hum of heaven
dying in her ear.

Testimony

I knew then there were infinite possibilities.
The world was catching fire.
Leaves turned one by one to flame.
I saw my life clearly, in an instant:
I had travelled by train, the long scarf
of its smoke the colour of your hair.
Once, the conductor turned his head to look at me.
His eyes told me he knew.
I travelled by foot the rest of the way.
Someone else had planned this journey.
Someone knew what my life was for.
I am here now. This is my story.
Lift your head and I will tell it to you.

The Night of My Conception

This is the dream that has recurred
all my life. It is the farm
I love and long to return to, and know
            I cannot.
It is no place I can find in this life.

They are still young,
            my mother, my father,
the trunk they carried off the ship
hunched and weary in a corner
of the cabin they built together.

The hearth logs lick the flames
            of their desire,
her dress rumpled on the floor,
his hat hanging from a peg. In the loft
where I will sleep in the bed
he will make for me,
            I hover, listening,
the night pregnant with stars,

the plow horses' thunderous feet
            quiet in their stalls,
the milk cow curled in the straw, all
waiting for the day I will reach out to them
with my curious hands.

Tonight there is a moon
            in the window
of the barn. But I remain
with the mother and father I will love
even beyond this life.

Like the rain
before it reaches us, like music
before the first note is struck,
I am the pearl
that will gleam inside her,
I am their song of songs.

And when the bright egg
of the sun dawns,
I waken and rise, wondering
where in the world they are now,

certain I would know them
by the sound their hands make,
their quickening breath,
their sighing just before sleep.

The Restive Angel

I have come from the other side.
I have crossed the field of battered weeds
and discarded tires, of razored glass and despair,
and I come searching for you. I am the voice
of the naked branch scratching the sky,
I am the groaning throat of stars, glaciers
of original light. I have touched the soles
of your shoes and tasted their dust,
I have counted your scars and hear
your hymns of grief. I carry your dreams,
the ponderous and prophetic, weighted
in my arms. I speak them into your ear
as you sleep. Beneath the insouciant moon
I hover in my lonely dress, my moth-wings
drawn to your lighted window, and there
I find you, burdened by memory, chained
by desire, your slow tenacity in scraping pen
against a page as if you chiseled words
in stone. I, who know only peace
and the inexhaustible light, come again
and again to stroke your silvering hair, marvel
at your thread-bare heart, your exquisite pain
here in the lovely, lovely dark.

The Small Gods of the Morning

Dawn, the lynx-eyed moon slides down,
a dim sun in the West,
              and the birds
cluster in their nests for the moment
of their rising. That pair of horses
hang their heads and wait
for the night to die its little death.

And the bones of deer and bison lie
beneath their skins of soil,
              fluted, sharpened
into what a hand could make
to be of use, render to stone:
an image of itself and of its universe.

The house you wake in sleeps,
just as the one you made
              in crayon as a child,
slept on its sheet of white,
a white house, the bright grass
at its feet, the light waking

behind trees holding their breath,
and the small fountain
you have fashioned in a bowl
pours itself out again and again,
              one leaf
lying happily at its depth.

The rose you set into earth
has begun to think once more of roses,
         and the cats
place themselves at the door
because they know you will step out,
walk down the path singing

whatever hymn you devised
in the furious clatter of your being.
And now the sorrel gelding
         rings the bell of the gate
with the hard fist of his hoof

and thus begins his prayer
that you come down
         because he knows,
and the cats, raising their tails to you, know
as rose, water, the trees' stony arms
         and the moon, all know.

You are a god, and all your kind.
Always so have you been.

Exile

*. . . the Lord God sent them forth
from the garden . . .*

Genesis 3:23

The gates stood open for eternity behind them.
Even at this distance, the angel's wings flared.
They thought in the hills they might quench
their nagging thirst, but day by day, they grew no nearer.
Ever since the naming, he had been insufferable.
The children, of course, didn't get along.
She combed the naked ground in search of food,
but whatever she happened upon, they devoured
in an instant. Their hunger knew no bounds.
Nights they huddled against the cold as the animals,
newly wild, encircled with floating eyes,
and the angel's wings hovered at the cerulean rim
of their horizon, the wilderness grown over
with a loneliness like nothing they could name.

The Darkest Place

Again she has found the darkest place,
            where she curls
like a quiet animal, where she knows
no one can touch her.
                    I find her
the moment I'm not thinking of her,
when I'm occupied with ordinary chores.

Plaid dress, princess collar,
            brown clip biting her hair.
I lift her up, hold her on my hip
and say, *they are not here now
                    and cannot hurt you,*
and I carry her into the light

where we can have a look at each other,
            girl and woman,
ourselves in the face of the other.

We are in this together. I tell her,
*see the rain on the window —
            how it carries your sorrow,
            how those leaves in the yard
have laid their thin bones down —*

I place words in our shoes, and we go walking.
*Silence. Mouth. Rescue. Heart.
Broken. Mend.*

                    Returned,
we stand in our stocking feet, tossing
            each word into the sky,
forgiving each other
                    over and over.

– II –

This Tree

Tonight, smoke rises over Buenos Aires
where the ghost of my childhood
wanders the autumn streets
and breathes the scent of April dying.

I hear shuffling from a dark portico
and know it is my own girl-self
shadowed in a dingy dress,
feet grimed with the city's detritus.

She has buried the memories
of those whose hands found her
in the night, and now no one
gives away her hiding place.

She is weary of holding out
her palms to strangers. She awaits
a dawning in her heart — the name
she bore when she was a bird

who combed the night and sang
the mornings open —
the name no one knows but God,
the name even she has forgotten.

The sky tosses back its long light
from street lamps and restaurants,
the sky flickers with lightning
but does not sweep the streets with rain.

The little black autos of Argentina
hold their eyes wide as a cat's
and race through the *calles*; the colliding notes
of a tango pour like a hymn from an opening door.

Child, I am your mother. Dream the sky.
In sleep build your wings. On fallen leaves
I pen messages for you. For you
this tree have I planted.

No Ordinary Place

I turned to look behind me
and saw the long road of my life.

Now I lead a secret existence.
I fill pages with all the things
I can't tell to anyone.

They sway like tall pines around me.
The moon climbs among their branches
        like a barefoot girl
straining for a glimpse of the sea.

Now the wind whispers
        stories in my ear.
It says my life is not what I believed.
It says this earth is no ordinary place.

And God, that lonely child,
                I've seen him
tossing winged seeds into air,
turning round and round in his bewilderment
as they sail back to earth.

Now I can't tell heaven from an ordinary day,
or heaven from hell, or my left hand
from my right.

To all my questions come answers:
Turn around. Look closer.
See where you have already walked.

And the stars, oh, the stars —
everywhere,
everywhere now, there is singing.

Daily Office
eight fragments

for Cecilia

1

Ripe berry, you,
naked and damp
with birth,
we brought you home.
I held you in the crook
of my arm, your new
mouth yawning,
your mewling cry. Snow
and the frozen
stars. From what far
world did you come,
and did you bring
this loneliness?

2

Tonight the jasmine
blooms for love
of the moon.

Trees, what tears
you let fall, what bells
you toll.

3

We sleep, we dream,
and memory unfolds,
scrapes at the house. The folded,

the unfolded, the life
and the death. Owl,
give away your darkness,
become the moon
and sing.

4

These slow nights of winter,
my little soul opens
and closes her wings.
She is grieving heaven,
her dream, mourning what
has died, what
is not yet born.

5

The light said, "Rise."
The morning said, "Choose."
And so I rose and walked
            to the sea,
the vast crowds of stones
already gathered.
And the sea, seeing them,
spoke. And the stones
murmured among themselves.
I understood little
but clouds changing
the sky, sea
changing the shore.

6

I fell from heaven

7

Morning grows into noon
and a woman
reads aloud. She knows
the book by heart, loves
the delicate curve
of the words,
little wrens, restive birds.

It's my voice, that bell I'm hearing.
I stand apart, heaven-fallen,
stranger to earth.

8

Sun's procession — a choir
of one. Moon's manna of frost
on grass — oh, what silence!

This daily office.
This awakening to light.

Like I Told You

It's like I told you, sometimes I live
not wholly in this world:
you know, a person can slip through
            the sheer fabric
of what you think this life is made of,

and just because you can't see it,
doesn't make it not there —
            the smallest tear, for instance,
you step through
            that leads
to nowhere you have ever been

and drags you toward itself,
            like the afternoon
I stood on an empty road
made simply of earth, the scent of earth
            rising to my nostrils,

a few stones scattered at my feet
and no other living thing I could see
to the thin line of horizon,
            only a bird
lifting the song she had just made,
            new, in her throat,
into the blue shell of the sky,

that seemed to call me to turn,
walk deliberately into a field of ripe wheat,
            the solemn and golden heads
full with their own strange music, and I,
            walking into it,

the wheat covering me above my waist,
and nothing I could see
        but the burnished heads shining
in the sun, reaching to the sky
            and the sky
bending down so low
they touched each other, when I knew
something was there —

a pair of yellow eyes, the wild
watching of one who had not been seen
        for many years
and was presumed no longer to exist,

and at the moment of my thought,
        the eyes had gone,
and there was no hollow in the wheat
to tell me it had come, that we
had beheld each other's eyes,

and I wondered then
        if I had seen it at all,
not another soul in the field
to tell me, too, about the eyes,
        the tufts of fur
inside its perfect ears, the stare

        that said it knew me
and had known me all along,
and you begin to look around, wondering
        where you are
and if you will ever get back
to what you know as the world,

but you do somehow,
because you can't stay there,
that's all there is to it,
         you must go home
and do the small things you do
that make up your life,

         and by doing them
put the day to bed
and call forth the night
                  in its vast
and unexplainable darkness.

Seeking and Finding

Birdsong
at the window.
A Tallis choir.
And just off the train

reddened with rust,
Dawn —
with its briefcase
and its newspaper.

Now you rise and search
for the poem, which is
the world,
singing itself —

wild, quick-winged,
with its memories
of night, the walking
trees, the moon

whose powerful paw
splashed light
on your forehead
as you slept.

Fence. Branch. Wind,
you say, naming what is
out there,
but find it, finally,

inside you,
little scarlet bird
that has trilled all night
a melody

in all its variations,
quicksilver
as a snail's trace,
fierce as barbed wire.

Such stubborn music, this
second heart
beating in your chest.

A Table in the Wilderness

for Cherrie

The spoon he lifts to her lips
holds a sun, the soup
I made from memory.

Around the table as we eat,
our arms touch.
We hold her in this net.

She is waiting to climb
into earth
where her room waits,

where the clocks are set
to a different hour,
and many are called,
and many chosen.

She will rise and climb
into the sky,
become a sparrow
with sorrow in her beak,

she will be lamp and shadow
in our empty houses,
will lie down
in the loneliness of stars.

We will search the night for her,
our faces shining, bewildered moons.

Tongue-Cut Sparrow

The child begs for the same story
night after night. She waits
beneath the white-starched sheet
in her bed beside the window, full open
           to the caught air,
unstirred leaves of the mimosa.

She pulls the sheet to her face,
           sniffs its clean,
and waits for her mother to come,
open the book, and begin.

Beneath the telling, her mother's voice,
the child wonders why
the old woman cut the tongue
           of the sparrow
fluttering among the bamboo,

and so in her days, the child
           sings for the bird.
She sings to the old woman
and believes the magic in her singing
will turn the old woman
           gentle and sane.

           She sings
after her mother closes the book
and rises without kiss or touch
and descends the stairs
           of her madness.
The child cups her hands,
breathes onto the sparrow
           and holds it to her chest

when the mother's rage
sends her hiding under the bed,

into the night of the closet,
            or high in the downy
blossoms of the mimosa,

and the little common bird
quickens its breath
until calmed in the curl of her fingers.

Always she vows
        to protect the bird.
She strokes the timid head,
feels the heat of its sides
                    on her cheek
and sings, believing
that the song, if sung perfectly
over many days and nights,
        will lift her mother
from the black room of her mind,
will lead her into light.

This Journey, Child

The child grew old
watching her parents remake the world.
They looked into her eyes and told her
what she saw did not happen,

as though in a moment the moon
                    turned its back,
leaves clambered up from the dirt
and locked themselves to the tree,
as though petals scattered by night's rain
        retook their places as the rose.

All the things that did not happen
collected in the dark place
                    beneath her bed
and entered her dreams as she slept.
Someone calling and calling,

her father, alone in a village far away,
whose name she counted
on the fingers of her small hands,
whose heart she held in the cup
                    of her small heart,
the father who whispered like wind
among the silken blossoms
of the mimosa, *The journey, child,
will be long.*

Beyond hills, and shadow,
on the other side of the rain,
girl who tumbled
        from God's coat pockets
into their hands, their need, the barren
ground of their love,
                I promise you
this journey will be long,
your true home another country
between morning and despair,
        between trespass and grace.

Child, speak your truth.
        There is no night
that you were not first born into.
        There is no sky
that is not already inside you.

Astonished Heart

I lay down at night and wakened
to the darkening of the world.

Beneath a sky of slate I chant
the liturgy of autumn, light
grown weary after its toil
of ripening, coaxing
      the myriad blossoms open,
the wheat to turn to gold.

I read the gospel according to trees.
It says: *Give away*
      all that you have,
make yourself destitute, bereft,
but first you must become as fire.

This is the first lesson.

From childhood I learned
the proverbs of rain
and of her sister, grief,
the frail pages stiffened
      from weather:
Grief can drown you.
Rain returns all things to earth.

This is the second lesson.

Once there was a child,
someone's daughter.
She folded her grief
      into paper boats,
sent them out on the water.

She folded her tears
        into paper birds
and let them fly from her hands
into the rain-dark sky.

The birds had eaten the path
        to her lost father.
She left bits of bread wherever she walked,
that he might come.
She held the last crust in her fist,
and when she slept she tucked her fist
            beneath her pillow.

She named him Wind. Starry Night.
She named him Rain on Parched Ground.
She prayed a small girl's prayer.
She made him into light, a candle
that flickered and made shadows of itself,
and she recited the parable
            of light:
There was once a love made manifest
in a crust of bread
crushed in a child's fist.
        Eat, child, eat,
that you become as flame.

I lie down at night and name the darkness.

You didn't know, my Father, you didn't know
            the years of my hunger.
My fingers curled around you.
I held you under my pillow
near the compass of my heart,
north star of my longing.

So much I keep there still:
the frayed scarf of your voice,
the curious little birds of your eyes,
mountains, rivers, the creased
       and faded map
I didn't know I carried.

I lie down and hear the wind
sing its hymn to the dying light,
unlock the leaf from the tree,
fray the tattered cloth of the sky.

Give away all that you have, it sings.
Take your grief into your hands,
bless it, plant it in the earth.
And there will come a living thing, born
       of soil, and rain.
It will bud and blossom.

This, the final lesson:
the parable of the astonished heart.

Hummingbird and Warrior

This hummingbird
will not die again;
your careful hands
have made him as though alive,
and all the birds come
to pay him homage.

You have placed him
in the hand of the Xian warrior
who is finished now, with battle
and spends his days
listening for wind's song
in the great bell
of the sky,

and keeps watch over his garden,
noting the changing face
of the moon, intimate
with her darker
and lighter moods.

He has grown gentle, this warrior,
and the bird, not afraid at all,
waits, quiet in his fist
so that the throat, colour of claret,
catches the afternoon light.

Like the last blossom of autumn,
this smallest of birds
has wakened his heart.
And God stirs,
always,
in the waking heart.

Tenebrae
Twelve Anthems Sung by the Earth

1. *Where Are You, O Mother?*

I suffer apparitions. Ecstasy.
Endless centuries
of grief.

Day and night
the lion moon
circles, finding nothing
to eat.

2. *Incomprehensible and without Beginning*

My cities of memory.

Mysterious astronomy
of the rose.

Compass
of the universe.

3. *Trisagion*

I am the crumbed table
on which the dishes
have yet not been cleared.

I thirst as the mouths
of leaves.

Wolf hunger
of the newly born
is mine.

4. *Celebration*

Geraniums in bloom
on the balconies
of Buenos Aires.

Mediterranean blue
seen from the caves
of Patmos.
Vincent's weeping yellows.

5. *Four Elements*

Scarlet: Picasso's Guernica.

Blue: Saskatchewan flax.

Gold: The hair of the sun.

Purple: Sky behind the racing moon.

6. *Joyous Light*

Always, somewhere, the sun
is a burnt sienna.

Chants of the desert monks
in the earliest hours of dawn.

The rattlesnake praying,
curled on ancient stone.

7. *My Heart Trembles*

A nomad, I walk
the shifting dunes
of Tamagesh.

Caravans pass. What loneliness —
their moaning wheels,
their belled herds.

The famine wind
flees through the trembling
doors of houses and of windows
frozen in their depressions.

The dead, underground, breathing.

8. *Have Mercy upon Us*

The chained and unchained.

Factory workers. Skin
on bone.
Those who must drink mud.

Cellists, poets,
and the architects of mourning.

9. *Therein Remember*

Those who have fallen
asleep. Saturn.
Jupiter.

Dear little Pluto, who has never
awakened.

How far to the end
of the universe.

What lies beyond.

10. *Nurtured in Love*

St. Gregory's fowl. Its feelings
toward the dove.

The dog who nurtured
a fawn, made a sacred space
on its bed.

How children in the streets
of Luanda, Saõ Paulo, Chicago
break a cracker into equal portions.

11. *Woe Is Me*

If only I could die
for you.

12. *Be Delighted*

The cicada's anthem.
Women carrying fruit on their heads.
The slow undress of autumn.

The Bandoneon Player

No more than ten he was, a Roman face,
dark curls in arpeggios descending his neck,
feet bare, trousers torn. Where he learned
to play that tango — love crashing into grief,
sweat into hunger — was anyone's guess. A traffic
light changed colour; the people darted across
like startled birds. And there in Avenida, Florida,
a couple began to dance. Down the block,
a woman dressed in white — white face, white gloves,
a human statue, turned her stone eyes toward
the boy. First her hands slumped, then her arms;
in her, some knowing opened like a rose.
And weeds bursting the tiles at their feet
grew beautiful in the Argentina heat.

All My Nights

All my nights have been one night,
all my moons, one moon.
The wind sings its one
eternal song
over all the world's days and nights.

I pack this suitcase with words,
phrases folded, neatly pressed,
send them into the light
and darkness of the world
that they may live their own lives.

In them, my prayer is answered,
that my father live forever,
and it is the owl instead
who calls to the night,
it is the gull who crosses the sea;

it is the blossom whose petals turn frail
as an ancient letter
in the slow breath of sleep.

Here I place his palms to mine;
I lift the page to his ear
        so that the moon
will sing of its cold love,

and all days are but the blue
arc of a single day,
and no one is lonely, and no one
is a rain-darkened road
leading out of sight.

– III –

Holding On

Why is my father standing
            in the apple tree,
feet splayed from branch to branch?
            Why this temptation
of my father to carry his seventy-one years
into the branches of this tree

and point his clippers at the sky
as if he could snip a piece
            of that blue cloth,
carry it into the house
and spread it over his bed?

Would it turn to darkness and stars
            as he slept?

I stand below, watching him,
            arms over his head,
shrouded in apple blossoms
cheery and wingy as angels,

and see him look skyward, past
the spring shoots racing
            heavenward,

and I want to *be* gravity, pull my father
            back to earth,
look him in the eyes with my grave face,
a little god taking him to task.

I want his feet on damp ground,
        my arms holding him tighter
than this tree which cannot fathom
        the word *daughter.*

It makes me afraid,
on this day of blooming possibilities
to see him stretching,
            seeming so intent
                        upon heaven.

My Father's Grief

I want to take away my father's grief.

I want to unravel the thread of it
from his shirts. I want to scrub
the dirt-black seams of it
from his fingernails.

I want to sweep it
from the doorways of his house,
wash it from the walls and hinges
        and window wells.

I want to capture the moth of his guilt
that has crawled inside his ear
and whispers its dusty word,
the shudder of its wings
        sibilant as shame.
I want to reach in and take it in my fist.

I want to quiet the river of sorrow
that gurgles its weary dirge
beneath his bed, his kitchen table.
        I will ask the willow
to quit her weeping.
I will point toward the sky, say,
See the moon ripening — there —
            in your branches.
Be now content.

I will call the little birds
to bring the lilt of their gossip
into the yard.
      I will call the crows
to carry the bonehouse of his sadness
in their beaks, open their wild
         blue-black wings
and drop it into the sea.

I will place the stones of the dead
beside the back fence
and I will sing them to sleep.
      It is enough now,
I will sing. *Enough.*

Go to sleep, you dead.
Leave my father to his life.

I will plant a tree whose blossoms
will burst and scatter
over the wet
        black earth,
and I will call each petal in turn
joy, light, peace,
until I have named them all,

until my father's grief is consumed
      as though by fire,
and I will strew the ash of it
over the sea.

Fragments

My shoes, blind boats,
this Braille road vanishing.

Out in the storm, pink petals,
sudden birds.

That horse in high grass
a whale in a green sea.

Hummingbird at the feeder,
its quick tongue vanishing.

I light one candle,
another in the window glass.

My prayer multiplying.
I am filling with light.

You had your watching face on,
my shyness vanishing.

Radio

I take your radio,
the one you found as a boy —
dials intact,
      no sound —
set it on an apple crate
in a corner of my mind.

Turning the volume full,
I hear the minute hammering
of a spider
      framing her web,
a mole shifting its whiskers
in the blind reaches
of its den.

A field mouse slips out
from beneath the cat's claws:
I catch the rustle
      of its escape,
the startled
wing dust of moths,
          and higher,
an owl's shifting eyes —
two black moons.

Horse Head Nebula
paws the deep
      ground of space
that hums its far,
unfathomable music.

Beyond your window downy birds
huddle on branches
complex as the lines in your face
                    as you sleep,
the boy in you sleeping too,

who listened at night,
            dials turned high,
worlds and seas pooling
            in the shell of his ear,
riding the tide of dream.

The Axe

I watched him swing the axe in the sun,
split wood into fine and finer pieces,
the leaves like gold coins scattered at his feet,
his hair silvered, shining, a bright thing
that would catch a crow's eye, or a daughter's,
who had searched all her life for him. Raising
his arms over his head, swift he brought them
down, and the wood crackled and startled into air
like birds in sudden flight. Watching,
I learned the strength of him;
it frightened me, too, the power of him
who could make the quiet wood fly,
who could gather the flown and fallen wings
and turn them into flame.

Bird Man

Now light pulls away from both edges
of the day, from windows, from open doors.
Soon, my father at the edge of his years
will feed the birds from his open hand,
his greying hair the colour of juncos,
and they will come — with their stripes and crests,
their wing bands, their bright breasts,
to alight on his shoulder, his finger,
quicken the midnights of their eyes and learn
the starry stillness of his song. As light
grows old, leaves flare and die, he grows young.
Could I become a titmouse, timid wren,
he'd purse his lips in a kiss for me,
magician to the small, the wingèd ones.

Luck

Luck is this road trip I take with my father,
the wheels of his car
            rumbling *hallelujah*
over the pock-marked asphalt.

Luck is rain pitting the windshield,
        holy water of our pilgrimage.

I curl the fingers of one hand
        around the smooth stone of joy.
The dashboard clock doesn't work.
            Time has stopped,
but joy lies content and warm
                in my palm,

while my father's brother, father, mother
fall from heaven
            to crowd the back seat
and point to everything that's new
        since they left the earth.

I send us south: left here, right, left,
and we arrive at my old house,
get out of the car, peer through the window
        to a child's room — mine —

but the child I was isn't there;
            she's looking down on us
from the broad branches of the mimosa,
dropping threads of mimosa blossom
        on our heads.

"Here he is," I say, "*him* —
the one you're looking for up there."

My father's parents lean on the car,
wave their hands at the heat,
         his brother
off having a smoke,

and when he crushes the butt
         under his heel,
we clamber in and drive on.

I ask questions that have no human answers:
      What is the map of grace?
Who is grief's daughter?
Is hope a bird with blue flame for wings?
      Is the sky its mother?

We drive north to my father's house.
      I want to see the boy he was
slip out the window and down the drain pipe,

the aroma in that bakery window just too much
for brothers already etching their bodies
      with hieroglyphs of regret.

At the church, we check in on the musty pews,
      the astringent sun pouring
through Jesus' startled hands.

The bent-backed, hound-jowled preacher
      opens a book, announces,
        Blessed are the travellers,
for theirs is the crumbling road,
    the blooming weeds,
    the starry shards of glass,

theirs the dust of the past
      and the mud of the present
clinging to their shoes.

We drive on into the night,
      all of us pointing at stars,

when his father, mother, his brother rise
each to a constellation
                  of shattered light.

For an instant I see my father
in a time to come, rise too,
      but his hands still hold to the compass
      of the steering wheel

where he turns the four directions
of loneliness and desire, hunger and grief,
      that tie us to this heaven,
hold us to the earth.

Pentimento

When I climbed down the cliff by rope,
a heron fished from a boulder below, stretching her neck
the way a monk in prayer
leans toward a page of chant.

A seaplane, blustering animal, took flight,
but did not distract her, nor did I,
nor the migrating clouds,
the massed choir of pines.

From their nest of twigs
a pair of eagles rose,
hovered in wind over the stone
crest of the hill,

and like the presence felt in a room
where someone has died,
I almost glimpsed
what I was before entering this world.

Reading by Lamplight

Sometimes my father is big.
Sometimes he is small.
      There are nights
when my father is young,
and days when he is old.

Tonight he is his father's
      father's father,
reading by light of an oil lamp
in this rough cabin.

The print strains his eyes.
He holds his glasses aside,
tilts the page to catch
      the light of flame.
He cradles the book like an infant
in his workman's hands.

If I enter the room and say his name,
what would it be?
Winter Moon? Wind-shaped Cloud?
      Rose past bloom?
And yet he is as perfect there
as the complicated arrangement of stars.

Tonight, wind circles the logs of this house,
forms the words on the page.
      His eyes grow weary
following their swirl. The words
do not want to be still.

They tell him how much time
he has left in this life.

They form a clock with recalcitrant hands;
they chime the hour
          with the owl's fluted song.

One day, they say,
he must leave his books behind,
his papers, the shapes his hands
have rendered.
          He will travel alone,
a susurrant sea, the night
a darkness without stars.

Little Parable

At this place in the story,
God climbs in your window
        while you sleep,
while the moon and the sea
pray to each other:
hallowed be thy name . . .

and God stands beside your bed
watching your breath rise
        and fall in your chest,
as it has without fail since your birth.

He opens his book of names
and pressed flowers fall
        from the pages.
The cats rub themselves
on the frayed hem of his robe

while God studies your scars
and whispers, *Don't believe*
        everything they tell you
of your own failings,

it's just that ancient sorrow,
        the same old stones
weighing your pockets down,
the endless failure
                of the blossom
to remain blossom,
of clocks to keep still.

The first morning is inside you
        waiting to be born.
And God sweeps the floors of your house
and gathers up the dust
which small birds carry to their nests.

All you see when you awake —
the moon setting, and the sea,
        and God's shadow,
rumpled as a cloak
at the foot of your bed.

My Father's Watch

counts the solitudes, restless hours,
quickening days, every small
birth and death
            of my father's life.
Each moment significant, each
must be counted:
the time between darkness
            and birds,
between waking and the dream
that walks backward into night,
the instant just before
            he pours tea into his cup —
my father's watch must keep account,
mark the ledger
of his accumulated years.

Its quiet ticking is the sound of dripping water
which is the first music —
            concerto for heartbeat,
continuous percussion of the feet.

Sometimes his watch
            counts back into memory,
and then my father's hair loses its silver,
the colour of moonlight
            on still water;
his hair grows darker, thicker,
and my father, briefly young.

But the watch will not keep still.
It counts the hours my father sleeps
                and each second
sleep stands outside the house
                and refuses to enter.

My father's watch, stoic, deliberate,
marches into the future.
                Iris swell and blossom
and dry like inky paper on the stalk.
Leaves uncurl their fists,
                become the colour of blood
and sail into air.

And the moon face of my father's watch
keeps counting,
                alone in its lonely task
as my father grows old
and the stars, like distant porch lights,
                switch on, and on.

Sewing

for Patrick

With needle and thread so fine
      I can't see,
you stitch the pond to the blossom,
leaves to their stems, stones
to the damp earth.

Your threads a thousand hues,
                  this garden
your coat of many colours
the birds fly to each morning,
            where they unfurl
the bright embroidery of dawn.

On your knees as though in prayer,
you carve rivers in a map
            of the known world
that furred creatures visit
and might mistake for Eden,
its curious god and his wide hands
pulling chaos,
         planting order.

And if you sing or pray
      to the small gods of stones,
or to the hand that ripples the water,
I won't tell. And if at times
you leave your body
      to view your creation
as our Father in Heaven looks upon it,
I won't tell that, either.

Both day and night are gates
          in and out of this life.
Our shoes dream dust and shade.
Our hands move like the shadows
birds make when they fly.

          And when I ask,
set down your stitching and tell me
of the past lives of roses,
and how Time tangles itself
in the basket
          where its threads are kept,
our past and future
impossibly knotted together,

then tell me again how this garden
          is a book of poems
the moon memorizes when you sleep,
and how you've wakened nights
and lain in the dark,
          hearing him
whispering verses to the sea.

-IV-

The Heart Is an Argument with Darkness

after lines by Patrick Lane

Among the bright shells
and the pennies

I went searching for you. The voice
I heard behind my head, fierce,
quiet, was my own soul singing
above the moving tide, over the stones
shining and wet beneath the moon. Already
she had flown to you on the other side
of the mountains, beyond the shadowed
face of snow. I wasn't afraid.
I have found and lost you many times
on this earth. There is no other way
to come home but by walking
past ponies grazing in their winter fur,
rusted skulls of abandoned cars,
past the unconcerned grass, boulders
in constant prayer. It is what I must do:
wash my face again and again in the stream
until it drips with the sun's light,
the soles of my shoes worn
to a holy O.

Teach me the stars.
The way to summer.

for Rob

You didn't choose me, I chose you.
I chose to come back. I missed darkness,

dogs barking all night, the lament of geese
on a journey they'll never know the reason for,

but fly because they must, because the sky
longs for the bells of their loneliness.

I wanted grief again, my back wet and cold
against the earth, your slender finger raised

toward each constellation, changed into the shape
of someone or some thing we have loved.

Around us, trees mapping their new buds,
green stars pointing the way to summer.

Who will explain the bones?

for Nancy

The delicate hand of a mole
our cat discarded on the path.

In January, all that's left:
the skeleton of last summer's leaf.

What my dog carries home. Once
it was a whole frozen turkey.

Winter trees lined with snow.
The stumps our slash fire didn't burn.

Tonight's sliver of moon.
When your body went up in flame.

Now you are everywhere, my sister,
and nowhere. In the air

inside that bleached skull of a deer
with spring grass in its eyes.

Beyond the veil, astonishment.

for Drew

My heart, blind fish, dreams light,
love, its oxygen.

My heart, little rabbit, has memorized
your smell, your handprint on my skin.

My heart, little snowflake, leaps out of sky,
dizzy for its own cold joy.

I can take a little boat across the night.
I can find you again and again.

How did we make a language only we understand?
I have known you a long time.

There is no end. Only a veil, illusion, a mirror.
Astonishment the oldest song.

This life vanishes.

Even my breath flies into the past.
At wind's touch, the bell shivers,
but, faithless lover, wind moves on.
And don't get me started on how many dead
we've laid in the ground. Long ago,
I climbed down from the sycamore
and became a woman. What
was the sense in that? And just last night
I touched your stubbled face in dream.
How like breath you vanished at dawn.

Twenty-one feathers in the blue jar
and you still can't fly.

But I shall sing
          to the bloodied dawn

and settle the stars
          into their nests

my darting eyes
          quick among the stones

and blossoms oh
          how I will dazzle you
                    with my song

You can never find that place

where you waited, little moth, just before
you fluttered into the womb of your mother,
and where you will wait for your body
to release its last held breath. Don't go
looking under stones, or sea foam, or petals
strewn at the edge of the road.
It is right behind you.
You can't turn fast enough.
Quietly it follows you,
picking the wildflowers
it holds in the small of your back.

The heart is an argument with darkness.

The rose is an argument with grief.
Birth, an argument with death.
Music, with silence.
The fence, with infinity.
Love, with finality.
My ragged shoes, with your distance,
the road a vehicle for longing,
the wind arguing with my hair,
this heart who has set her face
and will not give in to despair.

Deferral

At evening my father lays down his tools
while the sun sets the sea on fire.

Who among the heavens knows
why he heaped lumber in the yard
as he did when a young man, and now
my father, sudden maker
of a shed,
        is Noah building an ark
for his hammers and his saws.

Rain-tight, mitres snug. Plumb.
       It will outlast him.

The rains, when they come, will be long.
Destiny shook her head at me and said
at the appointed time, he must cross alone.

Then bring your lamps, your bundled flowers.
Bring lupines, lilac, apple blossom.
Leave your oars and your grief.

           See the waters blazing, lit.
The darkness may not have him yet.

Bread, Cup

Tonight I awaken
to the bright coin
of the moon.
Light and shadows,
light
and shadows.

In the field, the horses
do not graze
in the half-light
but stand, quiet,
looking out from the dark
stones of their eyes
as though this night
were holy.

On my windowsill
a red leaf
thick-veined as a heart,
the compass
of a snail shell,
the smallest
of feathers — abundance
of my wandering.

These are yours;
I give them to you:
the last detritus
of my lost wing,
my compass,
my heart.

Sleep now, my weary father,
you who have gathered the leaves

of years into your arms —
blood years, bright years,
the burnished coins,
the weighty stones.

Your little flickering birds
coo to each other
under the moon:
sleep, go to sleep.

At dawn
with their attentive wings,
they will watch
for the moment you appear
bearing their bread
in your hand, bearing
their cup.

First Light

Before the first light
my father rises and peers into darkness.
Stars provide the only light there is.
My father
rises in the still dark and goes out
under stars or into the rain
at the dying end of the night
and waits for the day to come.

Morning, and my father's eyes
witness the breaking
of dawn. Two fawns form out of the night
and follow their mother carefully
across the lawn.
My father knows the light will come,
and yet he rises before it
to see that it comes.

I want to believe it is my father
who brings the dawn.
The morning has no father, and cannot
fear all I know,
that a day will come
when he will not rise.
For now,
I imagine him going out into the cold
light of stars, into the dark,

the starry choirs of nested birds
waiting
behind the darks of their eyes
for my father's raised hand,
when the first music may begin.

Sparrow

I am so happy you have come,
first bird to the feeder.
I have waited all this time.

My downy-headed sister,
in that last rain and wind
I looked for you, dreamed
your nest of horse hair and moss,
heard that flock of pines cry out
to the predator storm.

I, your angel of bright and tiny suns,
of sunflowers' black tears,
hungered for the day
when the lost twins of your wings
would find each other like hands at your back
as you discovered the gift.

It is no easy thing to bear
the weight of another's offering.
All the long winter I have done so little,
yet the rose is profuse again with buds,
and again she will permit me to watch her
bare her dozen yellow hearts.

Sparrow, here is your gift. It is enough,
the exquisite cage of your bones,
the hymns you sing at dawn,
to make the tight red bud in my chest
unfurl its myriad wings.

Imperative

I found you in the season of clocks and burning.
I carried little in my arms but loss.
You, an ocean beyond my human beginning.

Something in me knew you were living
in the far world, calling. I dreamed your voice.
Year after year, that constant seeking.

Inside the bell, the wind was singing.
You walked through my nights like a ghost.
And what about the heart, alone, and counting?

—

And what about the heart, alone, and counting?
You walked through my nights like a ghost.
Inside the bell, the wind was singing.

Year after year, that constant seeking
in the far world, calling, dreaming your voice.
Something in me knew you were living,

you, an ocean beyond my human beginning.
I carried little in my arms but loss.
I found you in the season of clocks and burning.

Naming

What if, by *song*, you mean
the space before dawn
when the birds have yet
            to awaken,

and I mean clouds smoothed thin
by the palms of the wind?

And what if, by *dream*, you mean
the darkness before you open your eyes
and begin to change your life,

and I mean knocking on every door
            to find the one
whose name and face I do not know?

And what if, by *empty*,
            you mean *full*,
and I mean a breath opening its wings
to the morning?

And what if I name you *clear brook*
            murmuring over stones,
and you name me *little cloud*
            shy behind the moon?

Then let us drink tea in silence
            but for the song
of the liquid pouring from pot to cup
as a cat will leap from a fencepost,

while small birds lift into the sky,
      holding in their beaks
the words we don't need to say

which they carry to their nests,
placing *hand* next to *cheek,*
      tea beside *communion,*
separating *age* from *sadness,*

and like little feathered gods,
      proclaim it good.

ABOUT THE AUTHOR

—

Pamela Porter is the author of three previous collections of poetry: *Cathedral*, *The Intelligence of Animals*, and *Stones Call Out*. Her poems have garnered many accolades, including the 2010 *Vallum* Magazine Award for Poetry, the 2011 *Prism International* Poetry Prize, the Pat Lowther Award shortlist, and have been featured on Garrison Keillor's *The Writer's Almanac*. Her novel in verse, *The Crazy Man*, won the 2005 Governor General's Award, the Canadian Library Association Book of the Year for Children Award, the TD Canadian Children's Literature Award, and other prizes. M. Travis Lane has written, "Porter's poems are pervaded with a sense of grace, of mercy, beauty and benediction." She lives on Vancouver Island with her family and a menagerie of rescued horses, dogs, and cats.